D0671324

BEAMS OF PRAYER

I mean to sing to the Lord
All my life,
I mean to play for my God
As long as I live.
May these reflections of mine
Give Him pleasure,
As much as the Lord gives me.

(Ps 104:33)

Beams of Prayer

*Spiritual Reflections
with Edward J. Farrell*

Compiled and Edited by Lynn L. Salata

ALBA·HOUSE   NEW·YORK

SOCIETY OF ST. PAUL, 2187 VICTORY BLVD., STATEN ISLAND, NEW YORK 10314

ST PAULS

Library of Congress Cataloging-in-Publication Data

Farrell, Edward J., Rev.
    Beams of prayer: spiritual reflections with Edward J. Farrell /
compiled and edited by Lynn L. Salata.
        p.   cm.
    ISBN 0-8189-0856-4
    1. Meditations.   I. Salata, Lynn, L.   II. Title.
BX2182.2.F35   1999
242 — dc21   98-47378
                                              CIP

Produced and designed in the United States of America by the
Fathers and Brothers of the Society of St. Paul,
2187 Victory Boulevard, Staten Island, New York 10314,
as part of their communications apostolate.

ISBN: 0-8189-0856-4

Printing Information:

Current Printing - first digit   2 3 4 5 6 7 8 9 10

Year of Current Printing - first year shown

               2001   2002   2003   2004   2005   2006

DEDICATION

Beams of Prayer was birthed by
Lynn Salata during the 25th anniversary
year of *Prayer Is A Hunger.*

Lynn is the personification, the symbol,
the echo of all those who have read my books
over these 25 years.

This is all her doing, and it is
wonderful to behold!

And so, I dedicate this publication to her
and to all those who have enjoyed
and been nurtured by my writing.

Edward J. Farrell

TABLE OF CONTENTS

PREFACE

Beams of Prayer is a brief anthology of the eight published books of Edward J. Farrell, works as dynamic and compelling today as when his first book, *Prayer Is A Hunger*, was published in 1972. This synopsis is a gift to the followers of Father Farrell, and it will also introduce new readers to his work, inviting them to enter more fully into his gentle, contemplative spirituality.

Included here are reflections of a "world priest" known internationally as author, speaker, homilist, and retreat leader. Through inspiring words, Edward Farrell's message touches the hearts and lives of thousands each year bringing them a new sense of self, a new sense of God, and a new sense of themselves in God and of God in them.

Those who have come to know Father Edward Farrell personally — or through his books, articles, and tapes — recognize his gift. His words draw us to be all that we can be in Christ. He leads us to our own inner depths, to that holy place within where we find the Blessed Trinity awaiting us. He speaks to our hearts, lifts us up, and helps us to discover the unique path we alone are meant to follow. He offers us the understanding necessary to live joy-filled lives, lives that are satisfying, meaningful, complete.

In compiling *Beams of Prayer*, I selected some pearls of Edward Farrell's prolific works — readings that speak deeply to our hearts and depths. I have followed each reading with a corresponding reflection of my own, a personal psalm in the form of verse or prayer. Together, these paired reading-reflections are offered starkly and simply as contemplative fare for today. This is not a book to be read so much as a contemplation to be entered. It is a book to set aside while its beam enkindles something new in you. You will recognize yourself in page after page. You will feel invited to linger. You will discover yourself anchored more deeply in your best self and in communion with Father, Son, and Holy Spirit. And perhaps you will feel called, as I was, to open to your own reflective verse, to your unique beams of prayer.

Lynn L. Salata

To assist in further exploration of the works of
Father Edward J. Farrell:

SOURCES

Prayer Is A Hunger (Dimension Books, 1972)
Surprised By The Spirit (Dimension Books, 1973)
Disciples And Other Strangers (Dimension Books, 1974)
The Father Is Very Fond Of Me (Dimension Books, 1975)
Celtic Meditations (Dimension Books, 1976)
Can You Drink This Cup? (Dimension Books, 1978)
Gathering The Fragments (Ave Maria Press, 1987)
Free To Be Nothing (Liturgical Press, 1989)

BEAMS OF PRAYER

Call To Light:
Awaken To God's Presence

I am the light of the world,
anyone who follows me
will not be walking in the dark;
but will have the light of life.

(JN 8:12)

IN HIS UNIQUE WAY

JESUS COMES TO EACH OF US in His own unique way, in His own time. There is a gravitational pull, an endless current which we do not recognize which draws us beyond all things and people, but at the same time more deeply and freely into them. What patience, what passion God must have for us! He seduces us with the simplest of things — flowers, food, life, people, sun and moon, stars and sand, wine and bread. Each thing has its moment of transparency becoming a momentary sacrament of His loving presence. We are drawn into the beauty and extravagance of an early autumn day, and in this love of nature we suddenly discover a personal presence as if nature is loving us rather than our loving nature!

In prayer, word, sacrament, people, the contemplation of consciousness of Jesus enters into my consciousness. Day by day, His mind and heart, His love, experience draw me into Himself, into His way of looking at people, His way of loving them. God is more present in one person than He is in all of the sunsets, sunrises, all of the art museums of the world.

Can You Drink This Cup?, 16, 17

*H*e breathes His breath into me
>	again this day.
Not a casual breath, but
>	purposeful, resounding,
>	filling my lungs,
>	my very being
>	with Life.

I live today as I am created today.
>	Lungs filled with the breath of His lungs,
>	Heart beating the beat of His heart.
My eyes look upon His work, but it is
>	my soul which embraces its beauty:
That unfathomable, exquisite perfection
>	one can only experience and
>	never dream to describe.

I stretch beyond my own confines
>	to envelop all of Creation,
And in the act,
>	Creation folds upon me,
>	wafts over, encases, enwombs me
>	in its Life haven.

We are one.
I and Creation.
God and Creation.
I and He. He and I.
God slips into me as easily as my own breath
>	— as my own Life.

TOTAL PRESENCE AND LOVE

G OD IS NOT OUTSIDE OF US, apart from us, but within us. He is a presence, present to us. God is total presence and relationship. He is love, always bringing us to His fullness of presence and relationship. Prayer is an entering into His love, into His presence, allowing Him to enter our presence and love. God's presence is always a gift, continually being given. He cannot be otherwise for He is love; and each of us is an act of His love. We are His image, we are like Him. There is a secret, a hidden self in us; it is Himself.

Each of us is worthy of a little adoration. God "adores" us far more than we can adore God. God gives Himself to us in a way we do not and cannot give ourselves to God. God loves us as we have never been able to love one another. The secret power and mystery of God at work in us!

Jesus' love penetrates us, His presence enables us to have greater presence and consciousness, greater and greater love. There is no limit to the cumulative presence of love which sustains the deeper life. God's kingdom grows as we grow; we are His kingdom made visible, bearing fruit.

Disciples and Other Strangers, 84,85,87,88

$\mathcal{I}$ carry a secret,
A hidden self,
It is You.

All I have
and am
and will become
is You,
an act of Your love.

Even my gratitude
for gifts You lavish
for love You bestow
for breathing
and feeling
and praying
and being
is Your own.

Oh, that I might be
totally present
to You!
That I might
adore You
as You adore me.

OUR EMMAUS JOURNEY

E VERYONE IS ON THE Emmaus journey. Sooner or later Jesus catches up with us and walks and talks with us as we go our way. Something usually prevents us from recognizing Him, but wherever we are and wherever we go, He is with us even though we cannot name why our hearts are smoldering within.

Faith is a spark, God is the fire. The faith of a Christian today is personal and humble. Faith is always a beginning, a pilgrimage. Jesus is always ahead of us, and we are so often hesitant, if not reluctant, disciples.

We are fragile, earthen vessels, so easily shattered. In my weakness is God's strength, in my wounds He reveals Himself. It is not so much my faith as God's faithfulness. Maturing faith is attention to this living presence of God in the depths of one's being as one is drawn into Jesus' life of action for justice.

Gathering The Fragments, 11-12

$\mathcal{I}$ walk the road alone.

No, it only seemed so.
For here He is beside me.
        Stepping briskly with my step.
        Clarifying the point He just made.

        Has He been here that long?
        I failed to hear His preface.
        Is it too late to understand?
He stops mid-sentence,
        Laughing at my dismay.
"Here. Let me begin again," He says.
And once again, He picks up the pace.

Beams Of Prayer:
Seeking The Face Of God

Take it as a lamp for lighting the way
through the dark
until the dawn comes and
the morning star rises in your minds.

(2 P 1:19)

MYSTERY OF PRAYER

WHEN WE SPEAK OF Christ we speak of Him in Whom we "live, move, and have our being," out of Whom, and in Whose image we were formed, Who is our finality. We have a destiny. We can all experience this sense of destiny. We have, each of us, within ourselves the love that has not been expressed, the truth which has not been understood, the potentiality which has not been actualized.

Prayer is essentially a mystery because Christ is a mystery. Because we are in His image, we too are a mystery. We still do not know who we are. Yet we know that Christ calls us to pray, to enter into relationship, into personal union with Him, a union rivaled only by the hypostatic union. It is the call of Christ to know Him. And to the degree that we know Him, we begin to know who we are, and to know one another. It is by loving God that we come to love each other; and by loving each other we come to love God.

Prayer Is A Hunger, 15, 16

You are My seed, says the Lord.
I have planted in fertile soil.
You shall bear good fruit, for
    you are My chosen one.
Your heart shall overflow with love,
    with truth, with passion for My call.
Find yourself and you will find Me.

OUR JOURNEY IN PRAYER

PRAYER IS LIKE A JOURNEY, a journey which we can never cease making. It is like thinking, for each day we think again, never knowing when we may turn a corner in our thought and find ourselves in a world we had never perceived before. Each day we love, but we never love today exactly as we did yesterday nor will we love tomorrow in the same way as we loved today.

Prayer is, in another dimension, always a mystery of person; and what it is to be a person is forever a mystery. What is it to be a creature who thinks, a creature who loves, a creature who is willing to be with someone?

When we talk of prayer, when we talk of person, we are immediately involved in interiority, in inter-subjectivity, in inter-presence. It is intensely involving once we begin to experience the awe, the wonder, the mystery in our relationships to people. And there is, in prayer, the presence of Christ, the presence which we believe and affirm: the presence of Christ in sacrament; the presence of Christ in people; the presences of Christ which are, in some way, so unsettling to people today.

Prayer Is A Hunger, 11

Stranger,
When I look into your eyes,
I'm drawn to look again.
What is it I see?

Why so familiar?
Have I looked here before?

Who now stares back?
Who penetrates my heart?
Who lays claim to my soul?

Aah, yes. Now I see.
I see Him there.
Yours are His eyes.
So very familiar.

Yes. You and He.
You both look upon me
With my own eyes.

DRAWN TO PRAY

To PRAY IS TO NEVER GET over the wonder of being born, of being alive. To pray is to live in the profound gratitude that no matter what happens, we're ahead. More has been given than one could ever have expected. To pray is to be in reverence, in joy, in awe of some moment of each day. There are no perfect days, but there is a beautiful moment in each day that draws us into prayer, consciously or unconsciously.

To pray is to act on that suspicion that "in Him I live and move and have my being." Someone is always embracing me. Someone is loving me as I am worth being loved. Someone knows me as I am worth being known.

Christian prayer is not our effort to reach God, but a recognition of His incredible presence always with us, drawing us deeper into ourselves and into others. God became human to be with us and in us, to bring us together. Our prayer becomes Christian when we discover that our hunger for God is His hunger for us.

Gathering The Fragments, 20, 21

$\mathcal{A}$nd as I prayed:
"Oh, Lord, I long to live in You.
Take me into Your heart.
Never forsake me. You are my true Love.
You are my Light, my Life, my Hope.
I offer myself to You completely.
In You, I shall live eternally."

I heard His Voice clearly from within:
"Oh, child, I long to live in you.
Take Me into your heart.
Never forsake Me. You are My true love.
You are My light, My life, My hope.
I offer Myself to you completely.
In you, I shall live eternally."

LANDSCAPE OF REALITY

P RAYER IS A WORK, A DISCIPLINE. It cannot rest upon mere spontaneity. It does not come easily, just as being a person does not come easily. And prayer is the greatest, highest expression of us as persons. We will pray in the measure that we come to be persons; and we come to be persons in the measure that we pray. If we are persons, we are in contact with the landscape of reality; and Christ is the greatest Reality of the landscape.

Prayer always leads us to a deeper discerning of how we are before God and how He is leading us. The hope of any prayerful life is at every moment the loving discovery of God in the existential situation of our life. Our prayer never ends in itself but is to enable us to be in joy and peace and in deep quiet wherever we find ourselves. It is because He is always with us, and we have always a sense of His presence to us.

Prayer Is A Hunger, 16
Surprised By The Spirit, 92

$\mathcal{V}$istas.
So many.
Such glory.
Spread before me
Delighting my eyes.

Grand landscapes
    no cameras capture.
Bright scenes
  no words symbolize.

None to equal
    the vista
Of life seen through
    life in You.

Nor to meet
    the landscape
Of love known by
    loving You.

Oh, Jesus,
May You always be
The Landscape of
My Reality.

FROM OUR DEPTHS

PRAYER IS A WAITING. It is hunger; it is love. Prayer is a relatedness, and prayer is a stillness. A primary dimension of Christian prayer is receiving, is learning to listen. In prayer before Christ we must listen even as we are listened to. It takes time. We should have a place of prayer. And we should return often to our holy place.

Prayer is a growing; it is a discovering; it is a communion, a communion most of all with Him in Whom all things are. Prayer is an inscape, a totality of the universe experienced in the most minute atom.

Prayer, rightly understood, is an expression of the deepest levels of our being. Prayer for the Christian is always a response to the living Christ, to the living Person.

Prayer Is A Hunger, 17, 18, 19

Sometimes I'm so uncertain.
Do I really hear Your call?
You need someone grand for this
— And I am, oh, so small!

Sometimes I'm so uncertain.
Do You call me in the night?
A spark burns deep within me
— Mimicking Your light.

Sometimes I'm so uncertain.
Do You reach out for my hand?
With Your touch I am incandescent
— And, yes, with You I am grand.

DYNAMISM OF PRAYER

PRAYER IS NOT WORDS. Prayer is life always evolving, always moving. Prayer is always new. It can never be repeated, just as a moment of life can never be repeated. There is nothing old in God. There is nothing past. He is always new. He is always present, and in Christ everything has become new. Prayer is a constant experience of re-birth, of Resurrection, of new life given to us. This is the day no one has ever experienced before; no one has ever breathed this hour before now. The moment is utterly new, and in it, all of us become new. This is one of the great powers of prayer — that it is creative of ourselves. The deepest affect of faith is not in God but in ourselves. If we believe God, then it is we who change, we become the vision which He gives to us. We become the prophecy which He utters over us. We are transformed.

No one of us would ever dare to believe in ourselves as He believes in us. Our faith is more than our mind. It is creative of us. We can only become what we believe of ourselves. What He believes of us, we can only begin to dream.

The Father Is Very Fond Of Me, 87-88

*W*hat is this mystery called Me?
How does it feel to be Me?
  To live in My world?
  To experience with My senses?
  To think My thoughts?

Aah, to be enveloped in the essence of Me!

I hear You calling from My depths, O Lord.
You know a Me I cannot reach.
How much of Me is really You?

Aah, to be enveloped in the essence of You!

A Warm Light: Embracing Our True Self

Arise. Shine. For your light is come,
and the glory of the Lord is risen upon you.

(Is 60:1)

Believe in the light
and you will become children of the light.

(Jn 12:36)

TIME TO "BE"

S O RARELY DO WE HAVE TIME to be, to listen for the sheer joy of hearing, to feel the early morning. There is so little time that when we do take it to allow what is real to be real to us, it has almost an unreality. Each day God imprints on us and within us a touch of the infinite, a longing for life, a yearning for unending love; we know Him as hidden and distant yet visible and near. He calls us from one degree of awareness to another, from one sense of being possessed to another realization of it. I am aware of having a life lived within me which is beyond my reach but very present to me. Sometimes everything that is outward brings back thoughts of Him to me. Yet it is impossible to rest or reflect at that level or at that moment on these things because they are only reminders to me that He is not met in these things but in the life which is lived within me.

Surprised By The Spirit, 16-17

$\mathcal{I}$ have but this brief moment, Lord.
Stop all time that I might savor,
Not glancing back at moments past,
Seeking not some moment later.

Fix my eyes to catch its beauty,
My ears to capture its sweet song,
Senses living out its magic,
Heartbeat beating its steadfast calm.

Commemorate these priceless gifts —
Beauty and song, magic and calm —
Offered by this moment in time,
Moment not lost, yet richly found.

IN THE WOMB OF THE FATHER

How does one become a little child? How does one continue to be born into an eternal birth? How does one discover the new in the daily gospel? It is adoration which supplies the link to our thrust into the future. Adoration is born of the experience of sacramentality, of the sacred inbreaking to the ordinary of life. In every child the sense of the sacred and mysterious is intuitive and direct.

There comes a moment when one knows in deep anguish the infinite distance between oneself and God. And there is the other moment when one feels deeply immersed in what could only be called the womb of the Father, so total and peace-filling is the experience.

Adoration of God is a long, slow, life process of interpenetrating manifestation and discovery, a cumulative exploration experience toward an ever-expanding horizon. Adoration is a gift: yet God is apprehended only if there be action and response on our part. It demands time and patience, patience with ourselves, a waiting for God. It is not a moment, but a cumulative process. Each day we must come to Him, and wait, allowing Him to slowly deposit His presence in us.

Surprised By The Spirit, 28, 30, 31

*E*ach day I cross
To the Holy Ground —
that place where God resides.

I unstrap my sandals,
then kneel low —
head bowed, eyes low;
thus I await His call.

> Straining to hear
> His footfall near,
> Hoping to sense
> His divine presence.

Each morning I come,
each night I depart,
failing to realize:
To see God's face smiling upon me,
I merely need raise my eyes.

AWAKEN THE CHILD

R EVERENCE IS THE NATURAL virtue of the child. A child is always filled with reverence. Everything is so totally new, so fresh, the child is ever surprised. Try to remember the last time you saw something you had never seen before. In a real sense, this is our experience in every moment — everything is new. We so often fail to look — really look — at one another. Each day we all wear a new face, a face different from all the other days of our life. We need not only the time to look closely at our own faces or the faces of those we meet, we need the awareness of reverence that makes this deep looking a grace and blessing, a participation in God's vision.

We are all called to awaken the little child within ourselves, the child who looks at the world with wonder and excitement and an un-self-conscious reverence. We need that kind of reverence.

We fail to appreciate, to reverence, who we are and who it is that lives in us. And inasmuch as we violate the gift of the person God calls us to be, we deny others the reverence of affirming God within them. Jesus tells us that we must love God, and love our neighbors as ourselves. This demands that we first love ourselves and let ourselves be loved by God. Only then can we know what the genuine reverence of love is.

Gathering The Fragments, 15, 16

Child, you are my own — my beloved.
My joy comes in your happiness.
My delight is to delight you.
I shower you with gifts each day:
    a splendid, golden sunrise;
    a lush, lavender cloud;
    soft breezes to kiss your cheek;
    scents of roses or impending rain;
    the song of a lark and hum of a bee;
    the twinkle in another's eye…
How I lavish these upon you, my beloved, my own!

IMPRINT OF GOD

W HEN WE SPEAK OF the prayer of contemplation, we think of experiencing the creative act
of God ever continuing in us, filling us with being.
To experience this is an adoration, a continuing adoration given us only through the gift of the Holy
Spirit. Contemplation is the activity of the Holy
Spirit in us.

Contemplation is like holding a magnifying
glass to God long enough for Him to burn His im-
print upon us so that we never can forget His presence in our life, so that we become a burning bush.
Contemplation is looking so deeply into things and
people that we are continually being ignited by the
rays and hidden flames emanating from the splendor of God's presence in all creation.

Contemplation must be the goal of all our lives
because God is the end and peak of it, and that end
and peak must be contained in some way in every
action of our life. There must be the realization that
the Kingdom of God has already begun.

Prayer Is A Hunger, 20, 22
Gathering The Fragments, 12

I feel myself praying
a wordless prayer.

I am in love with You, Father.
I am in love with Your Son.
I am in love with Your Holy Spirit.

You never cease to awe me
with the wonder of You,
of Your extravagant giving,
of Your ongoing creation of me.

I feel myself praying
a wordless prayer
of my deepest love,
my deepest wonder,
my deepest gratitude.

I am enlivened
by the flow
of that small prayer
coursing through
the mighty river of prayer
always alive in me.

I see You
at the river's source
at the river's end
— silent, alone, and poor —
waiting for me
patiently and forever.

GIFTS OF HIS LOVE

E VERYTHING THAT IS HAS a language, has something to say. Everything that is has value and
meaning. Everything that is has a secret and is a
mystery. Everything that is has a history, has come a
long way. Everything that is is on a journey, has a
destiny. Everything that is has something to share,
something to give, something to express, something
to receive. Everything that is has something to speak
to you about yourself, to teach you something that
nothing else could teach you.

From the experiences of everyday things the
mind and heart are lifted to Him from whom all
things flow. Everything is a gift of God's love, goodness, wonder and beauty. Everything can be a sacrament of God, an epiphany, a transparency of His
presence. There is nothing in creation or man's experience that has not been an occasion of man's recognizing the power and presence of God. Our Lord
took bread and wine, water and oil, human word and
gesture and made of them encounters with Himself.
The sacraments and psalms can teach us how to pray
and how to discern His presence and love in all the
things of our day.

Surprised By The Spirit, 121, 122

Oh, that I might ever know
  Your Presence in every face
  Your Pulse in every heart;
That I might ever feel
  Your Breath in every breeze
  Your Touch in each rain drop;
That I might ever see
  Your Smile in every bloom
  Your Might in each sunrise.
And, oh, please grant
That I might view
  Life's beauty through
  Your Eyes.

TO THOSE WHO LOVE HIM

ONE CAN IMAGINE THE FULLNESS of Jesus as He experienced the inexpressible gratitude of men and women for all time slowly growing to an awareness and a conviction of resurrection with Christ.

His spirit is being released over all of humankind; truth, joy and peace are being poured into us. All that is human is eternalized; all that is divine is now ours in Him. He is to be with us always, giving us a taste of what He is now, what we will become. He is drawing us into Himself. Now He is ever present; He will not leave us friendless. Before the resurrection He was limited by bodily space to one house, one city, one person, one group at a time. No longer is He confined to a limited circle of human presence. He comes fully to all those who desire and love Him.

Gathering The Fragments, 60

*A*t times
when I feel
so limited,
so insignificant,
so helpless
in the face
of this world's strife,
I call to mind
Your Life.

My arrogance,
my frustration
are dampened
as I recollect
Your own
human experience:
    Your divine might
    reduced
    to mine,
    enduring
    restrictions
    inherent in
    flesh and bone.

Restrictions of time
Restrictions of space
So much space
to cover in
so little time.

You, as I,
Yearning to
move
beyond such
constraints.

Aah, to extend
Your hand
to heal
the entire
world!
But, alas,
the hand
touches
but one
at a time.

My hand
and Your hand
touching one,
then another,
and yet again.

Individually.
Together.
Healing all
the world's
hurts,
one at a time.

Easter Life:
Joy In Abundance

*And reflecting like mirrors the brightness of the Lord,
all grow brighter and brighter
as we are turned into the image that we reflect.*

(2 COR 3:18)

Then will your light shine like the dawn.

(Is 58:8)

EASTER LIFE

WE ARE WITNESSES TO THE resurrection no less than the apostles and Paul, for the risen Christ can be known only in faith. No one recognized what appeared before their senses. The only Jesus we can believe in is the risen Lord who draws us to Himself, giving us His spirit, enabling us to believe. If we believe, it is through His spirit. The spirit in us enables us to see the glory of the resurrection, the quiet hidden glory of His annunciation, birth, life and death now continued in water, bread and wine, oils, human words and hands, the sacraments of every day which transform us into a sacrament of Jesus.

Easter life! One moment of life would have been enough, one moment of love, of consciousness, of truth, of joy. But we are called to live all these moments without end. His resurrection has begun the parousia; the world to come is here; the kingdom is in our midst.

Gathering The Fragments, 60-61

And God
breathes
His Spirit
into each
small soul
igniting it
to Life.

Breath.
Spark.
Flame.

Life.
Love.
Joy.

His
kingdom
is in
our midst.

AS HUMAN AS JESUS

W HAT IS YOUR EXPERIENCE of the mystery of the Incarnation? How often great truths are given to us long before we can understand them and live them consciously. Great truths of the faith, handed down from generation to generation, remain for the most part so hidden, so un-understood, that when in a special moment a radiance breaks through, we are startled and overwhelmed. So, startle us, Lord! Overwhelm us!

Incarnation is a call to wholeness, to holiness, to oneness, to universality in its root meaning — being catholic. What is the totality of Jesus' Incarnation? He became everything that we are, except sin, in order to draw us into everything that He is. He did not simply become human; He brought a whole new depth and height and breadth to what being human is. Our call is to become as human as Jesus is — a human-ness that we can only call divine. Nothing human is unknown to Him, yet how much that is human was hidden from us until Christ became what we are. He cannot take just a little of us. He tabernacles in us. He pitches His tent among us, in us, and He opens a new universe.

The Incarnation invites us to discover that joy is the good news, that He has come that we may have life and joy more abundantly.

Free To Be Nothing, 99, 101, 107

*H*e comes to me
Bearing Life and Joy.

His Life.
His Joy.
To become
Life and Joy
in me.

Imagine.
Life and Joy
of the Almighty
deposited
in a mustard seed!

ENERGY OF DIVINE LOVE

THE WORD BECOMING FLESH has made the human mysterious, has given the human length and breadth, height and depth that it never had in itself. The divine has stretched the human. Incarnation is the Word about who God is; and, we are each a word of God. Within each one of us dwells the creative Spirit, dwells the energy of divine Love.

Incarnation is open to us; Christ is alive in His body — the Church. Christ comes alive in us as we become free enough to give Him our heart; and then we begin to recognize the One who is the Heart of our heart. Every time we act in such a way as to reveal God, every time we abandon ourselves into God's hands, we participate in Incarnation. Each time we celebrate the liturgy, the sacraments of the Church, we live the mystery of the Incarnation. And as we witness to Christ's life in us, we can feel ourselves to be one corpuscle in His blood, one cell in His body. How can He live without us? And living through the commemoration of Jesus' life, we are born into the mystery of His life in us.

Free To Be Nothing, 101-102

*C*ome, my Lord.
I feel Your Presence.
I am filled with
    Your breath,
    Your heartbeat,
    Your pulse.
I am warmed, enlivened by Your movement
    within my being.
You have wrapped me in the cloak of Your love,
    made Your breath my breath,
    Your peace my peace.
I am at once serene and anxious,
    quiet and raucous,
    still and trembling.
Nurture me with Your Word.
I hunger to be consumed by Your prayer for me.
Take my hand. Give me Yours.
Take my heart. Fold it into Yours.
    And treasure it,
    And nurture it,
    And breathe new life into it.
That I might be born into Your life,
That I might live Your Incarnation.

LIFE IN INCARNATION

I AM AN INCARNATION. I believe that I have been seized and caught, that I live a life that is beyond myself. There is a life in me that I can never adequately touch. There is an understanding and a consciousness, a prayer and a love deeper than myself and I do not know where it comes from. There is a new consciousness that is beyond anything that has ever been dreamed or touched by the human alone. In the Incarnation, the divinity becomes human and the human is taken up into divinity.

The mystery of Jesus' wholeness is emptiness, is kenosis. He emptied. He was free to be poor, to empty Himself out so totally He could enter into our brokenness. He became everything that we are. There is nothing human except sin that is unknown to Him. Everything human now has a new depth and a new expansion. Literally, the new creation is far more astonishing than the original creation, and yet it is hidden. The Incarnation continues to increase in every generation, and yet it will always remain hidden. It can never be touched except through faith. Not because it is not real, but because it is more real than the physical. In some ways it demands more faith, not less faith. Not only did He become human, not only did He come down to our level, it would have been enough that the divinity became human. But He stepped even below our level; incredible as it may seem, He became our food and drink. The ultimate validation and evidence of Incarnation is Eucharist.

Free To Be Nothing, 103–104

44

I close my eyes.
Relaxing
      into my own center,
      into the realm of being
      where only Good can thrive.

As always,
I find You there.
It is here You reside,
here You await my visit.

(How I ache!
The pang of regret
Knowing I've
kept You waiting
so long
— too long.)

At my first step,
You hasten
      to embrace me
      to swing me high
      to hold me close
      to beam Your delight.

From this inner place
Your life permeates:
      in me
      through
      and
      beyond me.
Drawing me to live for You.
Drawing me to give of You.
Drawing me to draw others to You.

Eucharistic Life: Window
On The World

*That life was the light of men,
a light that shines in the dark,
a light that darkness could not overpower.*

(JN 1:5)

ORDINARY BREAD AND WINE

JESUS HAD MANY MEALS with His friends, disciples, and with strangers. But the Eucharist was more than just another meal. The Eucharist is a love ritual; it is also a death ritual. Remember His death. Remember His love. The Eucharist is the sign, the manifestation, the visibility, the evidence of Jesus penetrating the whole world through His presence in us renewed daily, as ordinary and common as bread and wine.

Though common and ordinary as human life, the Eucharist is always more than it appears. The presence of Jesus is dynamic, radiant, magnetic, reconciling, unitive. Jesus was lifted up once and for all; we can and need to be lifted up again and again. And He is always with us. It is in the Eucharist we are crucified to the world and the world is crucified to us. It is in Eucharist we are resurrected for the world and the world is resurrected in us. It is in Eucharist that the radical, redeeming, reconciling love of Jesus continues and is actualized in our own time.

Can You Drink This Cup?, 37, 87–88

I am yours through Eucharist.
Through Eucharist you are Mine.

Come to My table where
I shall lift you up.
You are My sacrament.
You are My eucharist.

Always and forever
I shall know you
In the breaking of the Bread.

INTO HIS OWN DIMENSIONS

S LOWLY THE EUCHARIST takes us into Christ, like the ocean carries into itself a grain of sand, and He stretches us into His very own dimensions! The dimensions of the Eucharist are the universe itself. In the body and blood of Christ, we become one with each other, one with the earth, the world, the universe. The Eucharist creates relationships, family, community, making everyone sisters and brothers. It is not so much that we change but rather that we come to recognize and identify what He has already done in His Incarnation, Passion and Resurrection.

The Eucharist is the invitation to remember. We are always being dismembered; we are always being fragmented. We must gather the fragments together and we must remember who we are; otherwise, we will forget the journey.

Can You Drink This Cup?, 90-91, 106

You think you see, My child,
    but you are blind.
I alone can open your eyes.

Go. Wash away the clay
    of this world
Then your eyes shall
    behold sights untold —
Always there but hidden to you.

Go.
Wash.
Run.
Quickly.
Time is precious.
I want you to live.

Move out of darkness.
Come into Light.

EUCHARISTIC LIFE

THE EUCHARIST IS LIFE, our daily life that comes to us each day freshly made. Like our life, it is a continuum, yet like our life it is new and unique each day. We will, as we live our today, live it as we live Eucharist!

The Eucharist is an event, a collision of God with the human. He comes, He really comes to us. All of Him becomes ours, we become His.

He feeds me with His own hunger. He stretches me toward the limits of His own consciousness. I pass through the walls of the senses and the dimness of the mind across the world and grow more and more in the lives of all His people. And they grow into me and enter deeper and deeper into my consciousness, becoming "one body, one Spirit, one hope, one Lord, one baptism, one faith, one God and Father of all."

I live now, not I, but they live in me. His members, His people live in me and I live in them. The Father and all that He is and that is of Him comes into me and I enter into Him.

Prayer Is A Hunger, 65-66

Nurture me, Oh Lord!
You alone have the
    Bread of Eternal Life.

Stretch me.
Mold me.
Create the "me"
    You desire I become.

Come.
Live within.
And I —
    I shall live in You.

PERSONAL PRESENCE

W E CAN BE PRESENT IN MANY different ways. We can be present in a room or to a room; we can be present to a person or with that person. There can be physical presence and personal absence. We can be so present to ourselves that we are not present to another.

The Eucharist is personal presence. There is an incarnateness and presence limited in time and space. The Eucharist is a here-and-nowness, not an everywhere-ness all at once. The Incarnation took on limitations of time and place — Jesus was only one place at a time. The Eucharist is under a similar limitation — He is not equally present to everyone, everywhere — any more than we are. Wherever He is present, He is present as person, as relating, as interacting. Jesus in the Eucharist always affects our presence. Christ is present to us each in a unique way, according to our faith and love and according to His love and mercy which is unique for each of us. He is present personally as person to Himself, to the Spirit and to the Father. He is present personally to each of us as persons, as knowing us by name, calling us into being and drawing us on to Himself in glory.

Prayer Is A Hunger, 58, 59

*P*lease —
Forgive me.

Too often
my preoccupation
prevents
Your coming to me.

You wait
at my heart's gate
while I
turn to lame affairs.

They call and call.
You wait
   Silent.
   Patient.
   Full.

I am absent to You
while hurrying to quell
one empty call,
then another.

And yet,
You wait.

And when,
at last,
I turn my gaze,
Your whisper
fills my ears,
drowning the shouts
of all others.

AT HOME IN US

JESUS TOTALLY REVOLUTIONIZED prayer. No longer is it blind human groping for what is always beyond the grasp of body, soul and spirit. But He promised that He would come to us and His Father would come to us and They would make Their home in us. It would have been enough if He had only left His word with us, but His love was so immense that He could not say goodbye. And so He committed Himself to live with us and be our daily food and drink.

The Eucharist draws us into a new depth of prayer. Jesus feeds us with His own life, with His own breath, with His own spirit. The Eucharist nurtures us with the very prayer of Christ, with His own contemplation, with His life in the Father.

The Eucharist draws us into contemplation, to an even deeper consciousness of the Trinity. Each Eucharist deepens and activates the indwelling presence of the Father, Son and Holy Spirit.

Gathering The Fragments, 21

I
am haven
to God

To Father
To Son
To Holy Spirit

I
needn't
look far
in seeking
Him —
I merely
must
come
Home

THE ULTIMATE PRAYER

THE ULTIMATE PRAYER of Jesus is the Eucharist. The ultimate prayer of Jesus is "This is my body given for you; this is my blood to be shed for you." The most important command of Jesus to all of us is not simply to say this but "Do this in memory of me."

We must become His body broken, His blood spilled out for the life of the world. We have learned well His invitation to come and celebrate. It is only in our day that we are beginning to hear His command to go out and be the sacrament of liberation, the sacrament of reconciliation, the sacrament of salvation for the whole world.

We are beginning to recognize that His word over bread and wine is rendered ineffectual unless we dare to lay ourselves on the line, unless we dare to utter that prayer, that these bodies of ours are given not simply to Him, but to the world. Jesus never asked us to follow Peter or Paul or John, but He said always and everywhere, "Follow me."

Gathering The Fragments, 37-38

$\mathcal{D}$are I believe,
Could I presume,
To become His Body,
    His Blood?

The concept is,
        perhaps,
        too large
        for me
        to comprehend,
        to imagine.

And yet,
If not I,
        then who?

CONSECRATED IN EUCHARIST

THE EUCHARIST IS A MEETING with Jesus, an experience of God. The Eucharist is our deepest act of self-identification with Jesus. He is always present, always ready to give Himself to us and draw us more deeply into His hidden presence in ourselves and one another. Each of us brings a different world for Him to take, bless, break open, and give back.

Jesus consecrated His own life in the Eucharist and He invites us to do the same with our lives. No one can do it for us. The decision, the consecration, the transformation of our lives depends on us.

Jesus enables us to experience more deeply the gifts we have already received. He calls us to celebrate the Eucharist over our lives and our world. He comes to us in His risen presence to empower us with the same Spirit that He was given. He takes, blesses, breaks, and returns us. Then He sends us as He was sent to make disciples of all the people we touch in our daily world.

Gathering The Fragments, 45, 46, 48

I approach Him
    Quietly.
    Reverently.
    Humbly.

In my cupped hands,
I carry
My world.

As I raise it up,
He lifts me,
A communal sacrifice.

Taking.
Blessing.
Breaking.

And,
To my delight,
The world
He gives back
Is created
Anew.

WINDOW ON THE WORLD

Jesus' whole life was and is Eucharist, and it is into this totality that He calls us as His disciples. Jesus' life was about carrying divine life to others, divine life so deep that it will always be hidden. Jesus is dependent upon our presence to Him today. He can be present to others only through His cumulative presence in us. The Eucharist makes us new dimensions of the Body of Christ. The human presence of God in Christ — Incarnation, Eucharist — now continues in us. He draws us gradually into the universal consciousness, into His identity with all people.

The Eucharist becomes our window on the world, our door of union with the other human beings who inhabit the earth. The Eucharist is ultimately shared prayer, the communal experience, the corporate contemplation of the entire world. He has given us bread from heaven that we might become bread for the world.

Gathering The Fragments, 50-51

$\mathcal{I}$ find
I have
great power
to bring
   joy
    and
    peace
    and
    life.

But
I am
merely
messenger
bearing
gifts
of
His
Light.

The Gathered Beams:
Becoming A Friend

Come. Let us walk in the light of the Lord.
(Is 2:5)

It is the same God that said,
Let there be light shining out of darkness,
who has shone in our minds to radiate the light
of the knowledge of God's glory,
the glory of the face of Christ.

(2 Cor 4:6)

AND WHO IS JESUS?

AS WE READ SCRIPTURE, we become more aware that it is an autobiography, that we each answer the question: "Who is Jesus?", by boldly saying, "I am." We dare to believe His promise that we can do even greater things than He had done. But there is no reconciliation without love, there is no love without suffering. That great symbol of reconciliation, the washing of the feet, is so significant for when we wash another's feet, we cannot see their face. They could be anyone's feet. They could be His feet.

The Eucharist is the living incarnation of His prayer of reconciliation. Reconciliation has already taken place, but so many have not experienced it. And this is our call, this is our mission that we are to make disciples, we are to make hearers, we are to create a kinship. We are to love unconditionally whether one is worthy of that love or not. Reconciliation begins with presence. We are taught presence through the Eucharist, to render ourselves present to the people in our lives. Each one of us has an almost unbelievable power to create one another, to call forth life.

The Father Is Very Fond Of Me, 54, 55, 56

$\mathcal{M}$y friend,
When you look
        into my eyes
        as I speak,
When you focus
        your attention
        toward my pain,
When you lift
        me with your
        smile and affirmation,
You become Jesus
        raising me up;
God, the Father,
        creating me anew;
His Holy Spirit
        pouring new life
        into my very soul.
With your touch
I am transformed
— and I
    will never be the same
    again,
    forever.

THE LOVE OF GOD

WE ARE MORE THAN AN ACT of nature or an accident. We are not just a statistical probability; we have each been chosen to be in existence. Within each of us exists an act of love. We are each an existence of God. We are each a visibility, a manifestation of love. How does God love? We have just to look around. This is the love of God. We are each the love of God.

The secret word which we each carry within ourselves is that we are loved uniquely. We are each a whole new species, we are not just one among a thousand other roses. We differ as star does from star, as planet differs from planet.

The Father Is Very Fond Of Me, 126, 127

$\mathcal{W}$hat might have been
the precise moment?

What might He have had
in mind?

What plan did He foresee?

when God
purposefully fashioned me,
knowing
when and where and why
He would
love me
into existence.

THE EXTRAORDINARY REALITY

C HRIST IS THE FIRST SACRAMENT, the primal sacrament; and each one of us, in the reality that we are Christ, is this presence to one another, because faith comes only through people, only through persons. This is a reality which we are only dimly beginning to perceive — an extraordinary reality. Christ comes to us in His Word, in His Scriptures, in the active word of the sacrament; and something happens to us. The love of Christ changes us. We are different as persons because Christ really affects us as persons. We are constantly and continually being formed.

Prayer Is A Hunger, 13

I am Christian.
I am of Christ.

I walk His path.
I work His plan.

I give my eyes
    that He might
    look lovingly upon
    this world.

I offer my limbs
    that He might
    reach out to
    those in need.

I surrender my heart
    that He might
    love all creation
    through me.

I am Christian.
I am of Christ
I am Christ.

He creates me thus.

BELIEVE THE TRUTH

I F ONLY WE COULD BELIEVE THE TRUTH!

If we believe the truth that Christ as a Person is continually incarnating Himself in our life; and that through every Mass Christ really unites Himself to us, then we will expand and grow in His greatness. We will be given new eyes, new ears, we will be given a new heart, a new mind; and this will happen continuously in Christ.

What the first disciples discovered, what every disciple has discovered is how long it takes to believe in the truth, to believe in the love of Jesus, to experience oneself as the beloved disciple! To be a disciple is to be the beloved disciple. A disciple is chosen, to be chosen is to be loved.

What then is it to be a disciple? It is to experience being loved so completely that existentially we are incapable of being other than totally His.

Prayer Is A Hunger, 19
Disciples And Other Strangers, 14-15, 15

ow I hunger
for You, My Lord!

Even
in the course
of my every day
I yearn to know
You are near.

I am ever in need
of Your guidance
Your expression
of Love.

My moments
contain a
kaleidoscope
of feeling.
But
beneath all
flows the
knowledge of
Your
devoted
Love.

CHRISTIAN LOVE

PERHAPS OUR DEEPEST ACT of faith is to believe that we have God's heart, God's power to love. The deepest act of faith is not in the reality that God exists but in the reality that God loves me, knows me by name, that I have the power of His heart, His compassion within myself. But I will never discover this unless I exercise it.

Select a person who is in and out of your life and decide to love them. Christian love does not consist in finding an object who draws love from you. Christian friendship is not an accident of finding the right chemistry. Christian love is deliberate, it is chosen. I love people not because they are worthy of my love but because I have the capacity to love and to call to life, to create. No one of us will ever appreciate the power we have to give life to another. We are the image of God because we have the power to believe in someone. We have the power to create life in others. There is no greater gift which we can give to another person than our time, our presence.

The Father Is Very Fond Of Me, 59-60

I need only
look to nature
to see God's hand.

Each bud and sprout.
The song of birds.
All mountains, seas, and streams.
Every sunrise and sunset.
In these are portrayed
His might,
His song,
His peace,
His love of life.

But, oh, the wonder
of His work in humankind!

I need only
look to you
to see God's heart.

PERSONAL CREATIVE POWER

WE HAVE THE POWER THROUGH our presence to each other to create or destroy, to call to life or to diminish life. The power of our faith in someone else is almost incredible. Do you remember the first time anyone spent time with you, sought you out, the first time anyone said that they liked you or loved you? Do you remember the time when someone said that they were unimpressed with you, that they did not think you were much of anything? The human word has created the person we are at this moment and has created the hope of who we shall become. Each one of us carries deep wounds within us because of someone else's words to us, because of someone else's faith or lack of faith in us, someone else's hope or lack of hope, love or lack of love for us. Every person in our life has in some way created us or diminished us, opened us or closed us.

Each of us has an aura, has a field of energy around us. Our presence to others calls them forth or holds them at a distance.

The Father Is Very Fond Of Me, 90-91

$\mathcal{A}$ word of praise is a newborn star
penetrating the fabric of night
scoring the edges of darkness
to burst forth in blinding light.

TO LOVE, SUFFER, RECONCILE

THE GOSPEL CALLS FOR unconditional love which is to say it calls for unconditional suffering. Although the gospel puts no value on suffering in itself, if one loves, then one cannot escape suffering. The very meaning of love is to render oneself present even to those who do not choose us and to continue to render ourselves present over and over again. To reconcile is to heal, to forgive. When Our Lord forgave, it was not with a word or with a gesture. When He forgave, He took whatever even He found within a person, absorbed it into Himself, and overcame it with Himself. Nothing of that evil or sin remained. We are moved to keep peace by preventing the occasion, by separating ourselves from the very people who might touch the nerve cords within ourselves. We find it far easier to accept separation and distance, to adjust to the situation of coexistence. But that is not reconciliation, that is not where our prayer should lead us. It was Gandhi who beautifully summed up the gospel by saying, "The love of one person is sufficient to compensate for the hatred of millions."

The Father Is Very Fond Of Me, 52-53

*H*ow easy it is to forgive — slightly.
To dismiss transgression by
  moving it out of mind.
To loose one's guilt by
  foregoing their debt.
To avoid treating an enemy
  as they deserve.

But what of
  true forgiveness?

How difficult
  to tear down the barrier,
  to erase a transgression —
  totally and forever —
  from the heart.

IN FAMILY WITH ALL

IN PRAYER WE FIRST BECOME present to ourselves because it must be an "I" who stands before Him. We enter into His presence and He sends us forth. All of our prayer is an effort to receive the thought and truth of our mind into our heart, and from our heart into the marrow of our bones, into our hands, into our feet. We are sent and we are to create — to create an environment, an environment of understanding, of compassion. We are to create the possibility of other people becoming present to themselves, we are to become a center of communion, of community where we cease to be anonymous, where we recognize one another as brother and sister, loving others not because we need them, but simply for themselves. It is difficult to comprehend how totally we are called to create family and kinship, not just in terms of our immediate family, but in terms of every person.

The Father Is Very Fond Of Me, 53

$\mathcal{I}$ know with deepest certitude
　　that I shall never forget
That moment when
　　　I discovered my reality in you.

When all I'd been taught
　　fell into place.

When all I'd dreamed
　　became true.

When teaching
　　and thinking
　　and dreaming
　　melded into
　　the tangible you.

Time stood still.

Your thoughts touched mine.

My life unfolded anew.

All at that glorious moment,
　　from which
　　I would always
　　know you.

BECOMING A FRIEND

WE HAVE FOLLOWED JESUS when He invited us to His dwelling, we have offered Him the hospitality and simple presence of friendship.

How does someone become a friend? One does not create a friend or choose to have a friend. A friend belongs to the realm of gift, of mystery, of the call to take off your shoes for you are on holy ground. Friendship seems to happen because of the quality of cumulative presence that builds up through the lapsed time shared with one another. This is how our friendship with Jesus grows.

The curious thing about our friendship with Jesus is that it draws us into a deeper friendship with other people around us. We begin to see that other people are friends with Jesus too. There is something of Jesus and His love in every person. This is the mystery of Eucharist.

Gathering The Fragments, 65

*H*ow is it we have become so close?

At what moment did familiarity move
    into friendship?

What magnetic field first drew us
    and continues to bring us together?

How can I explain the fond thoughts of you
    which ease into my busy day?

Why is it I'd rather spend one moment with you
    than an hour with anyone else?

You, my dearest friend, belong to
    the realm of gift,
    of mystery,
    of the call to
    take off my shoes for
    I am on holy ground.

Disciples and Mustard Seeds:
Beaming The Small Light

*Your word is a lamp unto my feet,
and a light unto my path.*

(Ps 1:19)

*God called you out of the darkness
into his wonderful light.*

(1 P 2:9)

FISHERS OF HUMANKIND

ONLY JESUS CAN MAKE US fishers of humankind; we cannot make ourselves powerful. We must learn to be disciples of one another, to learn, to admire, and to grow.

In the past, specially gifted people seemed to be called to be disciples. Now Jesus seems to be calling very ordinary people, people who do not see themselves as anyone special, who feel that they know little and have nothing to share with others. But these are the very people that Jesus always calls. We become special when we begin to follow Jesus and allow Him to live more consciously in our lives. In surprising and simple ways, He is always speaking to us. He is at the heart of the world and at the heart of each of us, especially at the fragile center where we are afraid — of ourselves, of others.

Surprised By The Spirit, 105
Free To Be Nothing, 43

*A*ah,
At last, a few moments alone with you.
To enjoy your closeness.
To remind you that we are always together.
You in me.
I in you.

I have selected my special place in you.
The spot where I choose to reside.
It is at the very core of your being —
your center-most center.
The place where I can stand, lifting the
torch
of your pilot light.
From this vantage point I have a view of,
and a role in, every vestige of your life:
your thoughts, your ideas, your actions, your
prayer.

It is here that ultimate sharing takes place.
Here is where you can always find me —
waiting for you, living through you, living
with you.
Here there is light.
Here it is warm.
Here I am enveloped.
Here I am at Home.

ANCHORED IN FAITH

T RUE MINISTRY IS ROOTED in faith, in discipleship. True ministry compels one to discipleship;
true discipleship compels one to ministry. We are
born into ministry and it is ministry which draws us
into discipleship. What a paradox! What a grace!

The disciple is the one who is close enough to
hear and to respond to Jesus' deepest question, "Do
you believe me?" (John 11:26). Everything depends
upon my answer! My faith, my ministry, my lifestyle,
my prayer, is anchored in my faith in Him as present
with me, "always going before me" (Matthew 28:7),
"sending me" (Matthew 28:20), as the Father sent
Him (John 20:21). "This is the victory over the world
— my faith" (John 5:4).

A disciple is someone who experiences a presence, a joy, a peace within so deeply that they are
compelled to share it with others. A hidden mission,
priesthood, vocation lives in each of us.

Disciples And Other Strangers, 8, 9
Free To Be Nothing, 48

Anchored in faith,
I find presence.

Anchored in presence,
I find joy.

Anchored in joy,
I find myself.

Anchored in self,
I find mission.

Anchored in mission,
I find faith.

DISCIPLES AND DISCIPLINE

UNLESS WE DIE, THEN, THERE IS no birth, no maturity — no ability to work, to suffer, to labor, to bear in the body our wounds. We cannot be His disciple if our lives contradict His life.

Disciple and discipline are from the same root. In order to be a disciple we accept a certain discipline, enter into a particular style of life. If we accept the call of Christ, we learn how difficult it is to be His follower.

Inevitably our words are braver than our hearts. Have we not all experienced how difficult it is to possess deep faith? Our lack of it, our lack of power to attract, inspire and make disciples of the children of this generation — this is the world's victory over us — our lack of faith. "The Kingdom of God is not just words, it is power" (1 Cor 4:20). And it must be the power, the faith which speaks to the world today.

Surprised By The Spirit, 103, 106
Disciples And Other Strangers, 10

I am afraid.
Although ashamed
to show fear.

What if He asks
more than I can do?

Or worse:
more than I am willing?

I package my fear
in a tiny box
wrapped in color
with shiny bow.

"Here, Father,
I give you
my fear."

He responds:
A large, bright box.
"Here," He says,
"I give you
the skills,
the courage,
and the grace
to meet
Our task."

BREATHE THE DIVINE MILIEU

To BE A DISCIPLE IS TO BREATHE the Divine Milieu, to be in Christ, to hear always, "Without me, you can do nothing." It is to meet every person in the Holy Spirit, in the awareness that something more than me is what I want to give to you. What we believe becomes autobiographical, becomes a prophecy which we will fulfill. If we believe that we are "not much," we will become "not much." If we believe we are the "beloved disciples" we will become the "beloved disciples." If we act upon even our hesitating belief, "What if it is all true?", we shall begin to reap the thirty, sixty and hundred fold promised in this life.

When the experience of being disciples, of being loved so extravagantly becomes part of our deepest consciousness, it is overwhelming, even frightening. Inherent in the call to be a disciple is a call to change. No longer can we sing to ourselves, "I love my little world, I live serenely and safely in my private little world." We cannot be like everyone else. We can no longer ignore the question: "What am I ready to die for?"

Disciples And Other Strangers, 16, 17, 18-19

$\mathcal{I}$ am disciple,
the beloved one.
Head eternally
upon His breast.

Lungs,
soul,
essence —
stretched with
Divine Breath.

Desire to give
more than
I am
rages —
as fire
deep within.

Confident
to always
be laden
with loaves
baked in
my life
with Him.

THE COST OF DISCIPLESHIP

DISCIPLESHIP COSTS. In the command Jesus gave to His disciples to feed the multitude, to "Give them something to eat — yourselves," is shown symbolically that they were to be broken, to be distributed, to be eaten. This is the centrality of the Eucharist in our ministry — the giving of ourselves. We must be broken. We must give ourselves to Him. Only He can break us and distribute us and make us His bread. In the end, it is only the Lord Himself who can teach us to be disciples. Jesus commands, not with mere words but by His life. The only authority He has, that He has exercised in each of our lives is to create in us the desire to be what He is and to use our life as He used His life.

We have been loved so much that there is enough left over to give to others. Love enables us to see into the depths of other people's lives. This inner stream of God's love, like running water, always refreshes us so that we might offer a cup to others.

Surprised By The Spirit, 104-105
Gathering The Fragments, 16

I
emerge from
the stream
of God's love.

Where
I have been
Loved
into my
existence.

As
cool, fresh
running water,
I now spring forth.

Together In A Strange Land:
Our Cumulative Light

And they will not need lamplight or sunlight
because the Lord God will be shining on them.

(REV 22:5)

TOGETHER IN A STRANGE LAND

W E NEED TO BREATHE TOGETHER, to burn together, to recognize we are strangers in a strange land. Even as the candle or the wood cannot ignite itself, just as fire cannot sustain itself except in adhering, inhering to something, someone, so we need to be ignited, sustained by the depths of others, by their boldness, their passion, their imagination. We need the transparency of others, need others who show fidelity to the revolution. We need holy combustion, to be burning bushes which are not consumed. Only as disciples can we bring others to the inner melting point which releases the Spirit and His power.

The call remains, "Come and see." It is not simple; nor does it take place all at once. Rather, it is evolutionary. Christ will continue to ask us to go further, and we shall not know to what lengths He will call us. The first disciples were not aware in the beginning that they were disciples. They had no thought of ministry. It was enough to follow Him, to be with Him for the rest of their lives.

Growth in discipleship is to be sought, prayed for, struggled for. Discipleship becomes more and more free. The Lord will "seduce" only so far. The options become more and more clear, the temptations more and more subtle. Each decision to be identified with Him becomes more costly — it may cost me my life. There is no way to be a disciple except to the marrow of the bone.

Disciples And Other Strangers, 20,21

$\mathcal{I}$ am spirit
I am breath
I am fire
  for your light

You are boldness
You are passion
You are strength
  in my plight

Awakening
Enriching
Igniting
Our hearts

Disciples:
We are
More and more
Free

Responding
To holy
Combustion

Hand in hand
I lead you
Leading me

GIFTS AND REVERENCE

THE MYSTERY OF GOD'S GIVING is that He gives so much. Jesus gave His very life for love of the world. We are so constrained by our human limitations that we can love only with a small piece of ourselves. God cannot love except totally, completely, unconditionally. When we ask for expressions of His love, our very requests impose limits, and yet we are constantly amazed at the way He transcends those limits. We ask for a grain of sand and He gives us the beach; we ask for a drop of water and He gives us the ocean; we ask for life and He gives us eternity. God's gifts are His way of showing reverence for us; our reverence for Him must come in our grateful response to these gifts.

When Jesus walked this earth, He had a reverence for individuals that was truly an experience of love. And He has that same reverence for us as individuals today. In some way, the radiant glory of another person, of all of nature, is the glory of earth. Each one of us, in some mysterious way, is the glory of God. Through prayer we have to discern the radiant glory of God in one another. Each one of us is a kind of prism, a rainbow, a light for one another.

Gathering The Fragments, 16, 17

Out from the discarded,
The dregs of my past,
I stumble upon great worth,
My own gentle grace, beauty so soft.

The spark of new life
Ascends from the dead.
Blossoming. Bursting.
Spewing seeds of fresh growth.

Beckoning self to dimensions new.
Promising generation upon generation.
Creating within a creator,
A source of... and of again...
Hope.

LIVING IN HOPE

R EVERENCE IS VERY CLOSE to her sister, hope.
Hope does not force. Hope knows that time is
essential, waiting is necessary, patience is to be
learned. Hope can believe in time because it knows
that everything that is, is an excess. Everything that
is, is more than could have been expected, more than
is deserved. How good of God and how mysterious,
how wonderful and how strange for God to make a
dog, to make flowers (they seem so unnecessary), to
make blue skies and green grass. The excess of life!
There is no person that can demand anything to be.
Everything is above and beyond that which would
have been expected. This is the experience of hope:
from the experience and the reverence that *I am*, and
being overwhelmed with this mystery by the continuing mystery of the birth of what *we are*, there is a
hope that what is, will mysteriously continue to be.
One does not have to worry, one does not have to be
afraid, one can live in hope because the very act of
living is an exercise of hope.

Prayer Is A Hunger, 73-74

$\mathcal{G}$ift me with the hope-filled
understanding
That You await me patiently.
That I needn't make up for
    lost time.

Remind me that I have found You —
    and needn't seek anything else.

Remind me that what I've become
    and who I am
    are more than could be expected,
    more than I deserve.

Remind me that the strongest of trees
    slowly developed its strong, deep roots.

Let me thirst for time to savor new growth.

PERSONAL VALUE

WHAT IS THE VALUE OF ONE person? The silence and hiddenness of a person is as mysterious and secret as God's. Every person is an invitation to go deeper, to enter in reverence to the hidden presence of God. The contemplation and adoration of another person is inexhaustible, demanding ever greater depth of seer and listener. One must wait for the curtain between people to be drawn back before one approaches the inner door to the heart, the inner window of the soul. One must "hold" at a distance until the work of presence, listening, response has its cumulative effect in interiorization of the other. This mutual indwelling becomes a mutual creativity, discovering and releasing the power of the Spirit and the resurrection.

The Father Is Very Fond Of Me, 23

I am one of
extraordinary value.
And I recognize
you are as well.
We are priceless
because we are His.

We are vibrant
alive
glowing from
deep within.

Our incandescence
is boundless
Extending beyond
our confines.

Light and energy
surround us
and all those
we encounter.

A dynamic
peace.

In Him
we are at
home
within
ourselves.

Here is
where we belong,
where we are
meant to be.

Never alone:
Breathing
echoed by His.
Pulse
mimicked by His.
Sensations
shared as well.
> Joy
> Pain
> Happiness
> Grief

All lived
in conjunction
with The Other.

There is no point
at which
we end
and He begins.

Continuous beings.
Continuum of God.
Individually one.

ALL THOSE AROUND US

THE DEEPEST CONTEMPLATION next to God is another person. You are little less than the angels, crown of creation, image of God. Each person is image of God, a revelation, a transfiguration, a waiting for Him to manifest Himself.

The most beautiful, fascinating creature in all the world is another person — the face, smile, eyes, vibration, walk, voice. In a single face, in a few round inches there is incredible variety. Every face is another window of the world, transparent or opaque, in light or darkness. Every face is a new world.

How few people we know by name. How few we know in their inmost heart. In a simple look we see more people in a stadium, a theater, a shopping center than we will meet in our lifetime. Each person is a gift, joy, grace, sacrament of His presence. Each person is a message, a ministry, an invitation. We are all the Mystical Body, the communion of saints. There is an interconnectedness between all of our lives. People are a daily act of thanksgiving.

Celtic Meditations, 72, 74, 75

So long ago,
when I lived in despair,
I longed to have you near,
to hear your assuring word,
to know I was connected to you.

And so you came.

You came with so much more.
You brought your self
    as gift.
And delighted in my gift
    of self to you.

And that
was enough for all time.

I vowed to
never lose hope again.

And yet,
from time to time,
memory isn't quite enough.
I turn to look
for you and
your assurance.

So now,
I ask you
to rescue me
        Please
        once again.
Gently lay your hand
on my shoulder,
or whisper to me
of your love.

And I,
in turn,
will always be
here
to rescue you.

LOVE AND CELEBRATE

THE GREATEST CHARISM is loving, because only love reveals the truth within another person and mirrors this grace to them. Our greatest achievement is in human friendship, being with, to, and for others. Love is our greatest power. Each person has a unique love, a unique life shared, known by no one else. Each has a truth, a secret, a wish, a prayer.

We are learning to celebrate one another, learning to celebrate ourselves. Each day is a birthday! The truest celebration is to see each other through another's eyes, to discover the beautiful sensitivity in one another, to discover more of one another's grace. One of the most special of virtues is that of admiration. We do not admire ourselves enough, believe in ourselves enough. There is no one person who can fully appreciate me; each person uncovers but one of the colors of my rainbow. It takes a whole community to discover the rainbow. How much we do not see, do not appreciate in one another. Yet, we have each a unique, original appreciation of the other. We have each a unique, secret, insight. We need more moments to enjoy the celebration of one another. How long it takes to know another person; how long to let myself be known!

Celtic Meditations, 76-77

Love.

In my heart.
At the heart
    of every action,
    every treasured memory,
    each stirring thought.

My wait
    is wrapped
    in love.

Love, which
in turn,
wraps me.

In patience.
In confidence.
In peace.

Love
generating
love.

A Circle Of Light:
Living The Gospel

*Anyone who loves his brother or sister
is living in the light.*

(1 JN 2:8)

And Christ will shine on you.

(EPH 5:14)

NEVER ALONE

THE GREAT GIFT JESUS OFFERS to people is that someone cares, someone is there for them, that no one ever need be alone again. Jesus is the great teacher of friendship, the facilitator of bringing people together. Jesus is the great welcomer, the party giver, the gatherer of people, introducing people to one another so that they can come to know and love each other.

Jesus is the master friend-maker. And so His disciples are friend-makers. Jesus was always reaching out to meet people, to begin a friendship. He immersed Himself in their lives. He observed them closely and listened to them deeply. He loved them. He accepted them where they were and for whom they wanted to become. There was nothing negative in Him to touch off the negative in themselves. They experienced their hidden goodness in His presence. He was always "hatching" them by His warmth and affirmation.

Free To Be Nothing, 45

$\mathcal{T}$o forever be held in
    His rapt attention.
To be always alive in
    His love.
How glorious to savor this
    pervasive sensation!

Body cells alive
    vibrating, pulsing
    with His creative life.
A throb. A beat.
    Strong yet s-l-o-w.
    Rhythmic.
Yes, a tempo.
    Coinciding with heartbeat.
    Resounding outward.
    Encompassing

Being aglow, alive,
    always warm.
A blanket of blessing
    wafting all senses —
Wave upon wave on
    my innermost shore.

To forever be held.
To be always alive.
To dwell immersed in Life.

DISCOVER THE POOR

A MOST DANGEROUS, YET MOST common, delusion is to believe that we are already Christian, that we are spiritual, that we have already arrived, that we no longer have to move. Jesus is always going on ahead; we will always be in exodus, on pilgrimage. To be Christian, to be on a spiritual journey, is to live in tents, to be always breaking camp, to move, to be going from one metanoia to another, from one conversion to another, from manna to manna, from Eucharist to Eucharist, from poor to poor. Discovering Jesus is to discover the poor. Union with Jesus is solidarity with the poor.

Is Jesus to be with us always as the poor? There is no choice more obvious, more deliberate, more consistent than Jesus' decision to be poor. He chooses to be poor in every critical moment of His life — His conception at Nazareth, His birth at Bethlehem, as a refugee family in Egypt, life with His disciples and companions, as a fugitive from the Pharisees with a price on His head, His cross, His death and burial. His teaching to the multitudes was a handing on of Himself to the poor. His sacraments are poor, like water and desert bread. Without the poor, there can be no Christianity, no following of Jesus. Being poor is the first and the core of the Beatitudes, and the only beatitude in the present tense. "Blessed are the poor, for theirs IS the Kingdom of Heaven."

Free To Be Nothing, 94, 92

*O*h, Jesus,
grant
that
I may see
the
anguish
behind
each
face.

And, Lord,
please
bless
me
to provide
Your
gentle
healing
grace.

FREE TO BE POOR

TWO CAPITAL SINS OF OUR culture are materialism and individualism. The more things we acquire, the more we are cut off from one another and the more fearful we become of each other. We become so poor that we have to buy everything. Yet the most important realities cannot be bought, collected, or possessed by oneself. The deepest values are only experienced in sharing. There is but one path to Jesus and it is the same path which He took to come to us. He emptied Himself of everything so that He could become one with us. He has told us where we can find Him — in the sacrament of the poor. Being poor does not necessarily lead to love, but love always leads to being poor. Blessed are those who love enough to be poor, who become free enough to be poor with the Poor One.

We are called to love God first and then our neighbor as we love ourselves. How embarrassing to discover our neighbor is everyone... everyone who is poor. How embarrassing to remember that our neighbor is Jesus... is ourselves. For, who among us is not poor in some way — poor materially, poor in spiritual awareness, poor in the image of ourselves. Blessed, indeed, are those who love enough to love the poor, who become free enough to be poor with the Poor One!

Free To Be Nothing, 95, 97-98

$\mathcal{I}$ prayed,
"Jesus, let me know You.
Intimately — at Your core."

He answered
quite abruptly,
"To know Me best, know My poor."

A DEEPER DIMENSION

WHEN I WAS A CHILD I COULD outrun the little brook, leaping back and forth across it. Now life has become an ever-widening stream which outspeeds me, leaving me further and further behind. This experience creates in me a sense of poverty, a renunciation which I must accept.

There is, however, a deeper dimension into which one must enter if we are really to understand poverty. It is in identifying oneself with Jesus' human concern for the poor that one learns the full meaning of poverty. The poverty of another becomes mine. When another becomes poor, I am poor ... I am poor with the poverty of all.

Surprised By The Spirit, 37

*O*h, glorious
This day
To realize:
When I
Reach out
My arm
To offer
His gifts,
The hand
That accepts
Is His Own.

CHRISTIAN POVERTY

POVERTY, BECAUSE IT IS a Christian phenomenon, is a mystery, a charism, a grace.

Poverty is a relationship to the Father. It is an experience of providence. As Christians we are called to trust in the Lord. We do not believe that God will prevent evil from happening to us, rather we believe that even were we to be destroyed, we would still be called to trust in Him.

Poverty is a consequence of being in Christ. Poverty is a radiation of love. Poverty is not something which exists by itself, rather it is related to the ultimate charism of Christ which is simply His love for all. Poverty opens us out to our brothers and sisters. One cannot be poor and isolated at the same time.

Simplicity and poverty: purity and love, single-mindedness; the celebration of things rather than the consumption of them; a quality rather than a quantity; one flower rather than a bouquet. Poverty is consecration.

The Father Is Very Fond Of Me, 133, 136, 137, 139, 140

Love makes us vulnerable.
Opens us to hurt.
Magnifies rejection,
    separation,
    neglect.

How threatening!
To, at last, let down one's guard.
To trust unto abandonment.
To believe throughout all time,
Throughout all intervening space.

In you
I believe throughout all time,
Throughout all intervening space.
I trust you unto abandonment.
For you, I release my guard.
How liberating!

Love makes us vulnerable
Risks hurt.
Magnifies approval,
    devotion,
    concern.
Love makes us vulnerable.

LIVING THE GOSPEL

THE FULLNESS OF THE GOSPEL is given to everyone, the poor, the illiterate, the unemployable
— but they are not only receivers, they are givers,
transmitters, ministers of the Gospel. For who else
can transmit the Gospel but those who have experienced it, those who are needy, who are inadequate,
those who know their need of the Gospel, those who
have nothing else but the Gospel.

The Gospel is essentially for the poor, the cap-
tives, the oppressed, those who know they are in need
of liberation, of redemption, of freedom, of meaning, of value.

Can anyone hear the Gospel unless they are in
need of it? Will anyone hear the Gospel unless they
are ready to live it?

We cannot change the poor, but the poor can
change us. They can lift us up and we can become
with them co-heirs of the Kingdom.

Can You Drink This Cup?, 78, 79, 80

At last, definitive action
To move closer than arms' length:
I came to bring you the Gospel
To bring to your world new strength.

What I found was *your* gospel story,
Drawing me into the world you've sown;
I discovered the lack of boundaries
And a new love to carry back home.

Mosaic Of Each Other:
Our Dawning

But if we live our lives in the light,
as he is in the light,
we are in union with one another.

(1 Jn 1:7)

MOSAIC OF EACH OTHER

E ACH ONE OF US IS AN orchestra all our own, an orchestra in which there are brass, reed and wind, stringed and percussion instruments. We are constantly being played upon by the many people who come and breathe a moment in our lives, pluck a chord here or there, strike us in some new way. There is a symphony; there are notes that are being drawn from us each day. There are movements in our life that most of the time we are unaware of; there is an ongoing development and we need time to reflect upon it. We are constantly drawing one another, enriching one another. Every word that has ever been uttered by anyone is carried somehow within everyone. We are carried by everyone who has ever heard our desire, our hope, our longing. It is amazing how much of each other we carry within ourselves. We grow in the most unusual ways in people, ways which we would least expect. How we grow, where we would like to grow and when we actually find ourselves growing are part of the mystery of community. Sometimes our most idle word has been the most meaningful word in another person. We are a mosaic of each other.

Prayer Is A Hunger, 67-8

$\mathcal{W}$e are a mosaic of each other —
Each a piece of a greater collage.
We are energized in one another.
Together. Empowered. Involved.

With you, I live in strong kinship.
You teach and you share and I grow.
I'm amazed how deeply I meet myself
when I open to you and let go.

It's surprising how much of each other
we carry within our lives.
We stretch and expand in harmony.
Individually, together, we thrive.

ONE BRANCH

Each one of us is but a fragment of Jesus, one member of the body, one branch, one leaf of the vine. Only together can we grasp the whole. We need each other to discover the whole Christ, the whole person each of us is called to be.

When we have been touched by Jesus, when the Spirit is stirred up in the depths of our being, when we dare to own Paul's words, "I live now not I, but Christ lives in me," then we can no longer live for ourselves alone. I am compelled to share my faith with others. God's presence in me overflows into the lives of others and I become receptive to His presence and power in others. You are different from me but we were born involved in each other.

Gathering The Fragments, 12

*L*ost
In a vast and
   winding maze
Where I know that
   God dwells,
I walk resolutely
   announcing:
"Here I am, God."

Only the size of a
   mustard seed
In this cavernous
   spiraling space,
I relentlessly move on
   seeking Him.
"Here I am."

The seed I am
   begins to sprout
First height, then roots,
   and buds.
And so, I now recognize:
I am a branch in search of
   the Vine.

Winding.
Walking.
Upward.
Calling.
"My God, here I
am."

Seeking.
Persisting.
On and on.
Straining to
   see ahead.

My tiny leaves
   begin to
   unfold.
I see the more
   to this Maze.

In my search
I'd failed to
   realize
The path I walk is
   the Vine.

VISION OF JESUS

J ESUS SHARES HIS VISION with us. He wants us to see ourselves and our world as He sees us — as we are, as we could be. When we pray, Jesus lights His light in us so we can see. He lets us dream His dream. What Jesus dreams in us is the Kingdom of God.

No one else has my vision, my particular way of seeing what Jesus sees, nor do I know your vision, that which Jesus dreams in you, sees in you.

The Christian knows that their vision is personal and yet is not a vision to be lived in isolation. The inception, development and transmission of the Christian vision is always an experience with others.

Realizing Jesus' vision being dreamed in us is bound to change us. Imagine the dream the Father has for each of us. A dream so real that it becomes creation, a love so immense that it becomes Incarnation, divinization. Imagine Jesus' love and what He sees in each of us, that He could dream we could be like Himself. In Christ, we are dreamers and co-dreamers. We dream together with Him. He dreams in us, creating a new world.

Free To Be Nothing, 108, 136, 138, 144

*H*olding His hand,
  I relinquish my lead
Allowing myself to be led.

Leaving the confines
  of the life I have lived,
I find a new world in its stead.

The vision of Jesus —
 His Light lights our way.
The Kingdom of God is at hand.

I stand at the edge
  of His dream for me
And suddenly I understand.

AMBASSADORS OF CHRIST

WE ARE CALLED TO BE ambassadors of Christ. We are invited to be His Word to others. Evangelization is not one person, one thing. It is everyone, each in a unique way following Christ. Evangelization is a *community of disciples*, witnesses of Christ. Essential to the very mission of the Church, evangelization must bring the Good News into all areas of humanity, so that through its influence, humanity will be transformed from within and made new.

There is a ministry, a mysterious ministry in each of us. We do not know where it comes from — that call in each of us which goes beyond our own heart. It is His call to pray in depth, His call to evangelization. You have been given the Holy Spirit in order to recognize that call already given to you. Prayer reveals there is something more. We are compelled by prayer to go out of ourselves. The prayer of the Christian becomes mysteriously entwined with Christ.

"I am an evangelizer! Me... an evangelizer!" The evangelizer is not just anyone. The evangelizer is a person on a journey, a pilgrim, a small star in the darkness. Jesus sends the evangelizer into the midst of people as His Father had sent Him.

Free To Be Nothing, 52, 53, 56, 57, 59

A light shines from deep within
    — Deep within my depths.
It is peace.
It is wisdom.
It is love.
It is hope.

Also it is patient,
        humble,
        dedicated.

Each day its glow intensifies
Until I feel myself
    — my entire being —
Burning brightly.

As I travel on His journey,
My flame radiates through space.
        — I am a new small star
            in the darkness.

COMMUNITY AND REVERENCE

BECAUSE "IN HIM WE LIVE and move and have our being," each of us is truly an existence of Jesus. Our responsibility is to discover Him in one another, to enable Him to come to be. Community is always His mystery. Community demands reverence. Community means to discover reverence toward one another, to discover a deeper reverence toward ourselves. We need to discover more fully that mystery of what we are, because our sense of reverence and mystery toward ourselves will be the measure of our sense of reverence and mystery toward one another. What is it to experience reverence? — to be carried away by God, to be carried away by nature, to be carried away by another person? Reverence has something to do with holiness and wholeness. Reverence is a word that ordinarily is ascribed to God alone. We have reverence for Him and to speak about reverence in regard to ourselves is to speak of the relation He has with us and we with Him. It is a mysterious relationship — it is the mystery of God giving.

Prayer Is A Hunger, 69

$\mathcal{D}$o I remind you of someone else?

Often one's appeal
  is their calling to mind
  some other of the past.
    Their eyes.
    Their manner.
    Their laugh.

I ponder and know
  most assuredly:
    You remind me of
    No one I've ever met.

And yet —
You are so familiar.
    Your eyes.
    Your manner.
    Your laugh.

I have known you before
— And even before that!

Could it be
You remind me of me?

Light Of The Deeper Heart:
A Sense Of Spirit

No more will the sun give you daylight,
nor moonlight shine on you,
but the Lord will be your everlasting light,
your God will be your splendor.

(Is 60:19)

PERSON ENERGY

THIS IS NOT ONLY A REALITY, it is a mystery: that Christ does communicate Himself to us as persons, and thereby gives us the capacity to communicate ourselves to others in a more complete way. Christ's relationship to us creates fields or currents which ripple with activity so that we can have a radiation effect upon others and they a radiant effect upon us. It is as if there were generated "person energy." We energize each other. As Christ energizes us, and we energize others, it becomes a reciprocal never-ending, intensifying reality. All of us are members of Christ.

As St. Augustine tells us: "...And there shall be one Christ loving Himself."

Prayer Is A Hunger, 13, 14

Sharing my prayer with you, my friends,
  has always a radiant effect.
Alone I achieve so little,
  with you I'm profoundly direct.

My small, insignificant planning
  takes on momentum, life, and size.
The impossible seems quite easy
  when considered through your eyes.

Ideas ricochet around our circumference
  bouncing from mind to mind.
Building in purpose and detail
  becoming concrete in short time.

Let us meet in our prayer more often.
  Come rest here with every chance.
We'll energize one another
  for together our prayer is enhanced.

USING OUR GIFTS WELL

THE WORLD IS STILL GOD'S WORLD. Christ has loved us and called us. The work He has begun, the Spirit will bring to completion. He has breathed His Spirit into us, gifted us with new capacities and new intuitions. Taught by the Spirit, we can discern the things of the Spirit. Through the gifts given us we are equipped with inner radar and gyroscope, spiritual navigational tools. If we use the gifts well, we shall grow, they will develop. They are buds to be carefully tended; not all will develop at the same time and rate, for each gift has its season, its special moment in the life of the Spirit when it will come to fulfillment.

Surprised By The Spirit, 76

*E*ach gift has its season,
    its moment in life.
The Spirit brings
    fullness in time.

The pulse and the plan
    for creation
Ring loudly in each
    heart and mind.

Taught by the Spirit
    we set off anew.
If we use our gifts well
    we shall thrive.

Buds fragile call
    to be tended.
When ours bloom, we
    grow more alive.

INNER TRANSFORMATION

T HE SPIRIT EFFECTS OUR inner transformation, being born again. The Spirit stirs up, prods, lifts up; never sleeps, is persistent, wears us down, ever returns. "You hear its sound, but cannot tell where it comes from or where it is going." He has His own way of revealing Himself. He is always surprise. When we least suspect it, He is breathing in us. He awakens us, recreates a forgotten appetite, stirs up a lost hunger and thirst, gifts us with an energy, a facility, a freedom and "unites us to the Lord to make with Him one Spirit" (1 Cor 6:17).

The Holy Spirit is inclusive, all embracing, community-creating. He comes upon us not for ourselves privately but to enable us to *be* for others, to build up the Body. He builds the kingdom between us. He breaks down the strangeness, removes the barriers, and bridges the estrangement created by the cumulative sin of humankind. He enables us to perceive and discern the truth and light in each person. Our immediate rash judgments of others are countered by His unconditioned love and reverence of each person. We become open to the gift of each person. We become open to the gift of the Spirit in the stranger, to what may be lacking on one level being present on another. We begin to know what we see, in place of seeing only what we know. Instead of seeing only the outside, we develop *insight* and see from within.

Surprised By The Spirit, 111-112

*E*ntering gently my deepest self,
The Spirit descends upon me:
Bearing my own transformation,
Freeing splendor in all that I see.

With the Spirit's stirring and prodding,
In each stranger I find my friend.
Building the Kingdom within us,
We are each moment created again.

A SENSE OF SPIRIT

THE SPIRIT IS ELUSIVE, unobtrusive, as imperceptible as time and season, growth and age. Yet we have a deep sense of Spirit from the breath of our life, the pulse of our heart, the stirring of our conscience, the restlessness of our soul. In this, modern humanity is not far removed from the primitive. Aloneness, silence, darkness, sleep, and death touch us too deeply to allow us to forget the mystery of the absolute. How intuitive ancient people were in sensing that the Spirit was in all things!

The paradox of the Spirit is that we do not possess Him, rather that He possesses us, occupies us. We become "His," not He "ours." We are a grain of sand wanting to possess the ocean. He is the ocean that encompasses us. Yet for that incredible lifetime of Jesus, the ocean was contained in a human grain of sand.

Surprised By The Spirit, 108, 109

Elusive.
Unobtrusive.
Imperceptible as Time.

Breath of Life.
Stirring of Conscience.
Restlessness of Soul.

The Spirit of
God Within:
This is My Reality.

GOD'S WORK OF ART

THERE IS A PRESENCE IN ME deeper than my own presence, a prayer, an energy, a wisdom, a connectedness, a grounding that I have only inklings of — treasure buried in a field, a pearl of great price. There is something inside of me that can receive and respond to God. He draws me. He attracts me. He fills up my life. When you want to rest, to grow, to develop, shut the door, go into your inner being. Become present to the length and breadth, the height and depth within your self and you will learn, you will be reborn.

Immerse your being in God, in goodness, health and love, in beauty, joy and glory. You are God's work of art, His vineyard. There are no perfect days, yet there are perfect moments in each day. Treasure them! Treasure your connectedness with nature, with the universe, history, others, the whole world. Treasure going to the wellsprings where you are still being formed, still growing.

We need to be at home with ourselves, with others, with our God. When we discover our center and our connectedness, we come closest to sharing in the creating and forgiving power of God. Then we are always at home, no matter where we are, because God reveals His love by creating the home within me, within you, within all.

Gathering The Fragments, 79

$\mathcal{I}$ Am Helper.
  I prescribe.
  Give advice.
  Assist.
    People are drawn to me.
        Seek me out,
        Bring their stories.
    I draw them to me
        Seek them out,
        Draw out their stories.
  I recognize fear,
  Know hurt.
I Am Parent.
  Spouse.
  Friend.
  Kind Stranger.
I Am A Smile.
  A Touch.
  A Tear.
I Know the Needy
  better
  than
  they
know
themselves.

I Am Giver, Nourisher, Caretaker,
Understander, Forgiver
 who cannot give
            nourish
            caretake
            understand
            forgive
            Myself
  who knows not Self.
I Rush To Others
I Postpone Self.

Today I make the commitment.
Today I begin the journey.
   Brief? Long? Eternity?
To explore my inner shore.
Never to return.
   For when I reach Journey's End,
   I will find I have come Home.